EQUINE EXPRESSIONS

EQUINE EXPRESSIONS
FROM
THE KENTUCKY HORSE PARK

ROBBEE HUSETH

SALT LAKE CITY

First Edition

98 97 96 95 5 4 3 2 1

Text © 1995 by Robbee Huseth & The Kentucky Horse Park

All photographs copyrighted as credited

This is a Peregrine Smith Book, published by

Gibbs Smith, Publisher

P.O. Box 667

Layton, Utah 84041

Designed by Mark Stiebling

Edited by Dawn Valentine Hadlock

Front cover photo © Gemma Giannini

Back cover photo © The International Arabian Horse Association

Quote on pg. 49 is from MY HORSES, MY TEACHERS, by Allois Podhajsky.

Translation copyright © 1968 by Doubleday. Used by permission of

Doubleday, a division of Bantam Doubleday Dell Publishing Group, Inc.

Manufactured in Korea

Library of Congress Cataloging-in-Publication Data

Equine expressions / Robbee Huseth in cooperation with the Kentucky Horse Park.

p. cm.

ISBN 0-87905-653-3

1. Horses—Quotations, maxims, etc. I. Huseth, Robbee, 1954-

PN6084.H66E68 1995

636.1—dc20   95-4665

                                                                          CIP

Think, when we
talk of horses,
that you see them
Printing their proud
hoofs i' the
receiving earth.

—*Shakespeare,* Henry V

CONTENTS

KENTUCKY HORSE PARK, PHOTO © GEMMA GIANNINI

Enter the kingdom of horses. Surrounded by miles of white-board fence and towering trees lies the Kentucky Horse Park and the International Museum of the Horse. One thousand rolling acres of enchantment for horse lovers the world over features pastures and paddocks, arenas and polo fields, and barn after barn after barn. Over one hundred horses including racetrack and showring royalty call this paradise home.

The front gates welcome more than half a million guests and exhibitors each year. As you pass through those gates, the walkway leads to the visitors' center. To the right, a magnificent bronze of Triple Crown Winner Secretariat. To the left, the Man o' War Memorial. Within the visitors' center the film *Thou Shalt Fly Without Wings* prepares guests for the Kentucky Horse Park experience—and what an experience it is!

Called an "equestrian Disneyland," the park hosts over sixty major events each year, including the prestigious Rolex Three-Day Event. This is a theme park that combines the very best of man and nature.

Central to the park is the acclaimed International Museum of the Horse. A spectacular spiraling journey through history, the museum is "dedicated to telling the intriguing, romantic, and complex story of the horse and its relationship with man." Its impressive galleries and ever-changing exhibits win the approval of seasoned horsemen and neophytes alike.

One of the most striking exhibits is the Breeds Wall. From Akhal-Teke to Zebra, this beautiful display celebrates the unique characteristics of the different breeds. Using technology that seems worlds away from the antique sleighs and carriages in the next room, the Breeds Wall is a "two-story bank of illuminated photographs with computer terminals that provide information on the physical description, origin, and registries of sixty-three breeds of horse."

Outdoors the celebration continues April through October with the Breeds Barn and the daily Parade of Breeds where more than thirty representative breeds are shown to music and narrative by riders costumed to display each horse's heritage.

Here in *Equine Expressions* we have selected twenty-six breeds from the Kentucky Horse Park to create a tribute to the noble horse in its many forms. We hope you will join us in supporting this remarkable kingdom of horses.

Robbee Huseth

MAN O' WAR MEMORIAL, PHOTO © GEMMA GIANNINI

THE HORSE IN SPORT EXHIBIT, COURTESY OF THE INTERNATIONAL MUSEUM OF THE HORSE

11

"FREEDOM HORSES" BY VERYL GOODNIGHT, PHOTO © GEMMA GIANNINI

*Let us look beyond
the ears of
our own horses so
that we may see the
good in one
another's.*

-Old equine expression

A most fascinating breed of the equine world is the American Miniature Horse. This tiny equid is not a pony, but is in fact a horse in spite of the fact that it never stands more than 7 hands high. Attempts to create a miniature horse began about 100 years ago. The records of the breed's history are not complete, but the earliest examples of the Miniature were the result of breeding down small Shetland Ponies. About a century ago, the Falabella family established a practice of breeding for diminutive size on their ranch near Buenos Aires, Argentina. The Falabella Miniature is now recognized as perhaps the earliest breed of miniature horse in the world.

Today the American Miniature Horse consistently passes its small size on to its offspring. The breed has the long hair and tail of its founding ancestor, but shows the conformation of a horse: a refined head, proportioned neck, and short, yet clean, legs. While the Miniature appears in various solid colors, those with spotted coloring are the most favored. A beloved pet and an outstanding showman, the American Miniature Horse is growing in popularity throughout the United States.

Horses have hoofs to carry them over frost and snow; hair, to protect them from wind and cold. They eat grass and drink water, and fling up their heels. . . . Such is the real nature of horses.

—Chuang Tzu

There are few breeds that can match the abilities of the American Saddlebred Horse in the showring. However, this breed has a rich history far removed from the show world. Originally known as the Kentucky Saddle Horse, it was created to serve the needs of farmers and planters who often rode from dawn to dusk, supervising work in the fields. The horses bred for this role needed an even gait that would provide a smooth ride, and the stamina to work long hours. Sometimes the horse would have to work in harness as well. In addition to the breed's celebrated role in the showrings of today, it is also successful in trail riding, show jumping, and dressage.

The conformation of the American Saddlebred is elegance itself. The head is refined and relatively small, with large, expressive eyes, and ears held erect. The neck is long and the body is compact with strong shoulders and smooth, muscular quarters. The legs are long and clean and have excellent bone. The average height ranges between 15 and 16.2 hands. There have never been color restrictions for registration, so Saddlebreds come in all colors—solid and spotted. In addition to its conformation, the gaits and high-stepping action make this a breathtaking performer. There are four main divisions for Saddlebreds at shows: Five Gaited, Three Gaited, Fine Harness, and Pleasure.

... *through his mane and tail*
the high wind sings,
fanning the hairs, who wave
like feather'd wings.

—*Shakespeare*, Venus and Adonis

*A horse is a thing of such beauty . . .
none will tire of looking at him as
long as he displays himself in his
splendor.*

—Xenophon

The Andalusian originated in and gained its name from the Spanish province of Andalusia and has been highly regarded since the Middle Ages when it was the favored mount for European nobles. Its ancestors are the Iberian and Barb horses brought to Spain by invading Moors in the seventh century. The Carthusian Monks kept the blood of Andalusians pure, founding studs at their monasteries in Terez, Seville, and Cazallo during the late 1400s. The Andalusian was a major influence on the Lipizzaner breed in the 1500s and was used as a cavalry mount. Threatened throughout the 1800s by war and a devastating epidemic, the breed survived and today its appearance and action make it one of the world's most desirable riding horses.

The Andalusian has a distinguished appearance, often in shades of gray and occasionally bay, with a luxurious mane and tail. It is a compact horse with excellent proportions and usually stands about 15.2 hands. It has a flat or slightly convex nose, small ears, and its head is set on a substantial neck. The chest is quite massive, the quarters are lean, the legs are clean, and the action energetic. Known for its ability to learn and its superb temperament, the Andalusian is a remarkable companion. Of the Andalusian, William Cavendish, Duke of Newcastle wrote, "The Spanish horse is the noblest animal in the world."

So did this horse excel a common one
In shape, in courage, color, pace and bone.
. . .What a horse should have he did not lack,
Save a proud rider on so proud a back.

—*Shakespeare,* Venus and Adonis

My horse has a hoof like a striped agate
His fetlock is like a fine eagle plume
His legs are like lightning
My horse has a tail like a thin black cloud
the Holy Wind blows through his mane . . .

—*Navajo song*

Prehistoric men drew spotted horses on cave walls. Three-thousand-year-old Chinese paintings show spotted horses. The Appaloosa, however, is a distinctive spotted horse native to the American West with a heritage as colorful and unique as its coat patterns. It is descended from the horses selectively bred by the Nez Perce Indians who lived near the Palouse River in Idaho, Oregon, and Washington. Valued for its strength, speed, courage, and intelligence, the "Palouse Horse" was prized by other tribes and the white settlers that came to the Northwest. The name evolved to Appaloosa and the horse became what Meriwether Lewis called "an excellent race; they are lofty, elegantly formed, active, and durable." Following the Nez Perce war of 1877 the breed's future was uncertain, but in 1938 The Appaloosa Horse Club was formed to preserve, improve, and standardize the breed. Today over 500,000 horses are registered.

The Appaloosa is recognized by its spotted coat with patterns that include blanket, snowflake, leopard, and roan. The breed also possesses irregularly pigmented or mottled skin, an area of white around the eye called sclera, and vertical stripes on one or more of the hooves. This breed is versatile and competitive in events from western performance to show jumping. Often chosen for children's mounts because it is known to have a level head and even temperament, the Appaloosa wins hearts as quickly as its colors turn heads.

There is no secret so close as that between a rider and his horse.

—*old equine expression*

A prince is never surrounded by as much majesty on his throne as he is on a beautiful horse.

—William Cavendish, Duke of Newcastle

PHOTO © SHARON EIDE

26

ARABIAN

The Arabian is one of the most popular breeds in America. It is difficult to determine the origin of the Arabian Horse, since its history is clouded by legend and myth. The Koran says that Allah created the horse from a handful of south wind saying, "Thy name shall be Arabian, and virtue bound into the hair of thy forelock . . . I have made thy master thy friend. I have given thee the power of flight without wings." The Arab was clearly conditioned by its desert environment, where only the strongest and keenest survived. Its influence is seen in almost every breed of horse in the world. Today Arabians are used for pleasure and trail riding, dressage, jumping, ranch work, racing, and in competitions throughout the world.

The Arabian is characterized by its small, fine head, with a dished face and narrow muzzle, and wide-set, prominent eyes that are most expressive. The neck is long and arched with a clean, refined throatlatch. The body is lean but muscular, and the legs are strong with good bone density. The head and tail carriage are high and playful at liberty. In training, it is noted for its intelligence, but its hot blood will not allow it to suffer fools gladly. The coat is fine and silky. Purebred Arabians will feature coat colors of black, bay, gray, and chestnut, while half-Arabians may have other coat colors including Palomino and Pinto. The Arab typically stands between 14.1 and 15.1 hands. This most beautiful of horses possesses both elegance and endurance, excelling in long-distance competition.

It wasn't on the program and few were privileged to witness it, but one event at the 1975 National Show at Albuquerque was probably more beautiful than all the rest.

It came during the stallion finals, which were exciting to watch, with the animals all brilliant, stylish, and full of fire. Each animal had that something special that only an Arabian stallion possesses. To the eyes of spectators not familiar with the breed, the stallions might appear unmanageable.

Suddenly the class was over and the Top Ten horses placed. The National Champion was named, and then the ring was opened to spectators, enabling them to photograph, congratulate, or just admire.

In the midst of this excitement, a young Indian girl approached one of the stallions and asked the handler for permission to view the horse.

Permission given, she approached the animal. Onlookers caught their breath as she seemed to have no fear or show any caution in her movements. The handler (with an obvious expression of concern) looked on, as did many others, as the girl placed her hands on the stallion's mouth.

Her fingers worked with care, traveling up his face, around the eyes, ears, neck and on to his body . . .

It became apparent to all that the lovely young lady was blind.

The true beauty in the scene was not only the obvious pleasure the young girl felt in what she "saw," but this very excited Arabian stallion suddenly stood completely still as if aware of what was taking place.

Even as the young hands traveled the entire body, even down the back legs, this superb representative of [its] breed took it all in stride.

The handler stood with tears streaming down his face.

Thanking the man sincerely, the young lady passed to another stallion and another and another. With each new horse came the same unusual but beautiful scene, the breathlessly excited animal with tail high and nostrils flared suddenly standing silent as the girl examined him.

Tears ran shamelessly down the faces of most anyone who watched the scene, and with each tear was a tremendous sense of pride . . . pride for these wonderful Arabians we own.

Dixie Ryan from "Girl 'Sees' Stallions with Hands,"
The Arabian Horse Journal

The wind of heaven is that which blows between a horse's ears.

—*Arabian proverb*

31

From the time of Julius Caesar's occupation of what is now Belgium, the Belgian Horse has enjoyed a great reputation as a powerful and versatile animal. The Belgian Draft Horse is called the Brabant Horse in Europe and in America it is called the Belgian. The Belgian is the descendant of the type of horse used by knights as war horses. Richard the Lionhearted imported many Belgians to England and, when the mounted knight became obsolete, the horse's strength was utilized in agriculture. The Belgian has been exported throughout the world to improve local stock and it has greatly influenced the Shire, Clydesdale, Suffolk Punch, and the Rheinish Horse.

A docile horse and a willing worker, the Belgian usually stands 16 to 18 hands, but often exceeds even that tremendous height. The American Belgian has a relatively large head and short, feathered, muscular legs and large quarters. Its color is usually chestnut, sorrel, or roan with a white or flax mane and tail and white feathers.

Whether you regard the horse with awe or love, it is impossible to escape the sheer power of his presence . . .

—*Mary Wanless*, Natural Rider
(*Summit Books—Simon & Schuster*)

CLYDESDALE

The heavy draft horse most familiar to Americans is the Clydesdale. These handsome horses are frequently seen in large teams pulling brightly colored beer wagons, showing their flashing hoof action and coordinated strides. The Clydesdale Horse has its origin in Lanarkshire, Scotland, a district known as Clydesdale when this breed was developed in the mid-1700s. Improved roads permitted a shift from packhorse haulage to the use of wagons and teams. The Clydesdale was bred for this work in harness and has also been extensively used for farming in Britain. In America, the Clydesdale was primarily used in cities on express teams where its appearance and elegant gait were appreciated.

Standing 16 to 17 hands and weighing 1700-1900 pounds, the Clydesdale is not the largest of the draft breeds, but is the most recognized. The characteristics that distinguish the Clydesdale are its long, fine leg feather, smooth body, and coloring. It appears in bay, brown, chestnut, and roan, with the color accentuated by splashes of white that appear particularly on the face and lower legs. The most famous Clydesdales in America are the Budweiser Clydesdales owned by the Anheuser-Busch Company of St. Louis.

There is a touch of divinity even in brutes, and a special halo about a horse, that should forever exempt it from indignities. As for those majestic, magisterial truck-horses of the docks; I would as soon think of striking a judge on the bench, as to lay violent hands upon their holy hides.

—*Herman Melville*, Redburn

CONNEMARA

Legend has it that the Connemara Pony descended from Spanish horses, rescued from the Armada when the ships wrecked on the rocky western coast of Ireland in 1588. In fact, the Connemara's ancestors lived in Ireland for thousands of years, although some of the Armada's horses may have mated with local stock. It is certain that Thoroughbred and Arabian blood was introduced in the 1700s. By the 1920s, the breed was threatened by random breeding and the Connemara Pony Breeders' Society was formed to preserve the purity of these hardy grays. A key to the excellence of the Connemara Pony is the harsh environment in which it lives.

The body of the Connemara is compact and deep, yet not bulky. Its legs are short and clean with ample bone. With a handsome head, fairly lean neck, rounded shoulder, and abundant mane and tail, the Connemara stands between 12.2 and 14.2 hands. Its color is predominately gray, but sometimes black, brown, or bay. In spite of its relatively small size, the Connemara is known as an excellent hunter and jumper and it competes in dressage and distance riding. Connemara blood was used to influence the fine Irish hunter and today Connemaras and Connemara crosses are seen in top competition.

O thou, my milk-white pony, whose coat is as the moonbeams of this autumn night, carry me like a bird through the air . . .
—*Murasaki Shikabu*, The Tale of Genji

The Friesian is one of the oldest domesticated breeds in Europe. Native to the province of Friesland in the northern Netherlands, it is found in the art of the Middle Ages. The Friesian suffered a decline in numbers with the increase of mechanization on the farm and in transportation, and just prior to World War I there were reputedly only three stallions left. Introducing Oldenburg blood rejuvenated the breed, and the contemporary Friesian is used as a fine carriage horse. The beautiful Friesian seen in the film *Ladyhawke* created much interest in the horse in the United States. It is now growing in numbers and being used as a saddle horse as well as in driving competition.

One of the outstanding features of the Friesian is its very long mane and tail. These are never cut and often reach the ground. The breed also displays abundant feather and long leg hair reaching from the middle of the leg. The color is always solid black. The head of the Friesian is carried quite high and the face is most expressive. The legs and quarters are muscular yet smooth. Usually standing at 15 hands, the Friesian is small among the giants, bred to be smaller and lighter due to its splendid action at the trot. Known for its excellent disposition, this breed is finding an enthusiastic audience in the United States.

As art united with experience long
Taught him those lofty steeds in awe to hold.

—Nicholas Morgan in 1609 obituary of Sir Robert Alexander

The horse shall be for man a source of happiness and wealth; its back shall be a seat of honor and its belly riches, and every grain of barley given it . . . shall be entered in the register of good works.

—Mohammed

PHOTO © SALLY KLEIN

The Hackney was first bred in the county of Norfolk, England, which enjoyed a great reputation for breeding superlative trotters called the Norfolk Trotters or Roadsters. It is from this type that the Hackney descended, and in 1883 a group formed the Hackney Stud Book Society and the breed was officially created. The remarkable high-stepping gait of the Hackney made it a very attractive choice for show work and in harness to elegant carriages. The breed, as well as its smaller form known as the Hackney Pony, remains extremely popular today as a show horse.

The Hackney has a fine, small head set high on the neck with features expressive of its spirited nature. The neck may be crested and is rather muscular. Perhaps the best description still is that of Ophelia: "The first time I ever saw Ophelia . . . she raised her head, pricked up her ears and stood to attention, a living picture I shall never forget. She had a perfect head and neck, full of character going back with beautiful symmetry into splendidly sloping shoulders . . . she stood on a set of legs made of whipcord and steel, every thew and sinew standing out clear and distinct . . . I took my hat off to her . . ." —Alexander Gemmell on the 1884 Hackney mare Ophelia, as quoted in *The High Stepper*.

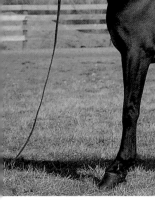

> When we think of the harness show horse we automatically picture the high-stepping Hackney. . . . They are noted for their action and only those who have ridden them appreciate the surprising smoothness of their high-actioned trot.
>
> —*Marilyn Childs*, Training Your Colt to Ride and Drive *(Trafalgar Square)*

Hast thou given the horse strength?
Hast thou clothed his neck in thunder?
He paweth in the valley and
rejoiceth in his might
He swalloweth the ground with
fierceness and rage . . .

—*Book of Job*

The Hanoverian Horse gains its name from its place of origin—the province of Hanover, Lower Saxony, in Germany. The bloodlines of the breed—the German war horse—reach back at least to the early Middle Ages. With the passing of the armored knight, the Hanoverian was bred with Spanish and Oriental horses to change its conformation for use as a cavalry horse. This new Hanoverian was capable of working under saddle, in harness on the farm, or drawing carriages. In 1735, King George II of England founded the famous Landgestiit Celle, which is to this day the official stud and training facility. Today the Hanoverian has been crossed with Thoroughbred blood as well as Trakehner. It proves a superlative hunter, show jumper, and dressage horse.

The Hanoverian's conformation reflects the influence of considerable cross-breeding in recent years. It stands between 16 and 17.1 hands and has a rather long head that has been refined by the Thoroughbred, a long, fine neck, a strong, substantial body with good depth, and well-sprung ribs. The withers are pronounced, the back and loins are strong, the quarters are exceptional with some flattening in the croup and a well-set-on tail. The legs are strong with large, broad joints.

ELECTOR ERNEST AUGUSTUS (1629-1698) ADOPTED THE WHITE HORSE FOR HIS COAT OF ARMS FOLLOWING A LONG TRADITION OF PREFERENCE FOR WHITE GERMAN HORSES. THE ELECTRESS SOPHIA BEGAN THE DEVELOPMENT OF THE ROYAL HANOVERIAN CREAM HORSES. THE HANOVERIAN CREAMS, ALSO KNOWN AS THE ISABELLAS, WERE USED IN BRITISH ROYAL PROCESSIONS FROM THE REIGN OF GEORGE I TO GEORGE V, WHEN THEY WERE REPLACED BY THE WINDSOR GREYS.

LIPIZZANER

With one of the most exciting and harrowing histories of any of the breeds, the Lipizzan Horses or Lipizzaners are the beloved white stallions of the Spanish Riding School in Vienna. Only the best stallions are selected for training, which begins at age four. Those stallions that demonstrate excellence at the school are eventually retired to stud at Piber, Austria—the government farm where modern Lipizzans are bred. Those individuals not suitable for the school often become excellent pleasure or driving horses. The Lipizzaner's name was derived from the location of its origin. In 1580, the Hapsburgs (the royal family of Prussia) first bred Lipizzans at the Imperial Stud in Lipizza, near Trieste. The horses have been used at the Spanish Riding School since its founding.

Averaging between 14.2 and 15.2 hands, the Lipizzaner has a relatively large head with small ears, dark, expressive eyes, and often a convex nose reminiscent of its Spanish ancestry. The body is compact with smooth musculature and a substantial frame. The legs are clean with small, hard hooves. Known for their docile temperament and intelligence, the Lipizzaners are born dark, but their coats turn white as they mature. One in 500 remains dark into adulthood.

NEAR THE END OF WORLD WAR II, THE CAPTIVE PIBER LIPIZZANERS WERE THREATENED BY THE BOMBINGS THAT HAD DEVASTATED EUROPE AND THE NOW-ADVANCING TROOPS. GENERAL PATTON OF THE UNITED STATES ARMY, A HORSEMAN HIMSELF, ASSISTED COLONEL PODHAJSKY AND THE SPANISH RIDING SCHOOL IN SMUGGLING THEIR LIPIZZANERS TO SAFETY. THIS RESCUE IS TOLD IN THE DISNEY FILM *THE MIRACLE OF THE WHITE STALLIONS*.

By reason of his elegance, he resembles an image painted in a palace, though he is as majestic as the palace itself.

—Emir Abd-el-Kader

48

From my earliest childhood it was my most ardent desire to ride, and I dreamed about it night and day . . . I wanted to ride and develop the horse's movements into dance and music . . . to ride and feel and learn from the smallest signs of the mute creature how to communicate with him, how to understand him and to create a language between horse and rider which would always remain simple, distinct, and constant.

—*Alois Podhajsky,*
My Horses, My Teachers (*Doubleday, 1968*)

One of the three American-bred gaited horses, The Missouri Fox Trotting Horse was developed in the rugged Ozarks. It was bred to answer the need for a horse that could carry a heavy load for long hours at a ground-consuming gait and, at the same time, a gait that was easy for both horse and rider. This gait is the distinguishing feature of the Missouri Fox Trotter, a broken gait in which the animal walks with the front feet and trots with the back feet. This shuffling gait, because of the sliding action of the rear feet, produced a smooth ride for the cattlemen, sheriffs, assessors, and many others who made long rides before the advent of good roads. While it was bred in the early 1800s, the breed did not become official until 1948, when the Missouri Fox Trotting Horse Breed Association started.

Today, the Fox Trotter is used for both pleasure and show. Unlike other gaited breeds, the Missouri Fox Trotting Horse may use no artificial means to accentuate his gait. The result is a lower, flowing, natural action at the flat-foot walk, fox trot, and canter. The breed stands between 14 and 16 hands, with a somewhat plain but intelligent head, deep chest, powerful sloping shoulders, and a relatively compact body. The limbs are clean and lean with large, flat joints and good hooves. The Fox Trotter is naturally surefooted and is most frequently found with chestnut coloring, though other colors are acceptable. With 45,000 horses now registered, this is a breed with a loyal and enthusiastic following.

God forbid that I should
go to any heaven in which
there are no horses.

—Robert Bontine Cunninghame-Graham
in a letter to T. Roosevelt, 1917

The Morgan Horse is a native American breed with an outstanding reputation for its elegance and versatility. While many breeds have found greatness due to their brilliance at a certain task, the Morgan's greatness is based on a variety of abilities. The foundation stallion, Figure—later called Justin Morgan after his owner—proved to be a prepotent sire who could haul logs from the New England woodlands one day and win an important race the next. He was unbeatable at any task. His most important sons, those that carried on the best Morgan qualities, were Sherman, Woodbury, Bullrush, and Revenge. Sherman sired the famous Black Hawk, who himself became one of the preeminent sires of the mid-1800s. Morgan blood has influenced many American breeds, most notably Standardbred, Saddlebred, and the Tennessee Walker. From the late eighteenth century to the present, the Morgan has been used under saddle, in draft work and carriage harness, in the showring, on the track, and as a cavalry mount in the Civil War.

The traditional Morgan stands 14.1 to 15.1 hands, with a small, refined head, short neck, and compact, muscular build that is smooth in appearance. The mane and tail are long, thick, and wavy. Short, clean legs display a dramatic gait with considerable action. Morgans are most frequently found in the colors of bay and chestnut.

Should you desire a mild-tempered horse which will work willingly under saddle, in light harness, on the range or trail . . . the proud progeny of old Justin Morgan will serve you.

—Pers Crowell,
Cavalcade of American Horses (*McGraw Hill, 1951*)

53

His ears up-pricked; his braided hanging mane
Upon his compass'd crest now stands on end . . .
His eye, which scornfully glisters like fire
Shows his hot courage and his high desire.

—*Shakespeare,* Venus and Adonis

PHOTO © SALLY KLEIN

54

His proud, bold and fearless style of movement and his vigorous, untiring action have, perhaps, never been surpassed.

D.C. Linsley on Figure, The Justin Morgan Horse
as quoted in The Morgan Horse

PHOTO © SHARON EIDE

This gem of a horse combines the qualities of the
Quarter Horse with stunningly attractive color patterns.
No two Paint Horses are marked alike, so to own one is
to own one of Mother Nature's original pieces of art.

—*Hardy Oelke*, The Paint Horse, An American Treasure
(*Kierdorf Pub. Co.*)

PAINT

The American Paint Horse is a breed distinguished by both its color and bloodlines. The Paint, like the Pinto, is described as either a Tobiano—in which white is the base color with patterns or spots painted in brown, black, red, etc.; or an Overo—in which the base color is other than white, usually sorrel or black, with the typically jagged pattern painted in white. This is a very basic description, of course. There are as many colors and patterns as one could possibly conceive in both the Overo and Tobiano Paints, and the breeders of these outstanding horses work through the most interesting genetics to create first, a superior horse, and second, a colorful one. The bloodlines of the Paint are Quarter Horse and Thoroughbred only. Pintos may be found in other breeds, including gaited horses and ponies.

The Paint without its color is identical to the American Quarter Horse, without the papers. It is often a stock-horse type with a small head, expressive eye, and an innate sense for working cattle. Paint Horse racing is popular in the United States, and you'll find Paints in many competitive arenas. The Paint Horse stands about 15.2 hands, and no matter its height, it is "big enough." It is compact, well-muscled, with powerful quarters and a long hip. The legs are clean and hard with short cannons and low hocks. The American Paint Horse Association, one of the fastest-growing registries in the world, was created in 1965 to provide a registry for these colored Quarter Horses.

58

Pure white he was, with a
cluster of red-brown spatters …
as though some Indian
paintbrush had created a
mystical design on his body. …
The wind blew aside his
foretop, revealing more
brown—a solid band across
his forehead, that continued
upward and out until it
completely covered both ears,
like a bonnet.

—*Marguerite Henry*, San Domingo,
the Medicine Hat Stallion *(Macmillan)*

The golden horse has been the choice of kings, queens, and emperors, the subject of artists' paintings, the pride of Queen Isabella's Spanish court, the treasured mount of ancient tribes, and the companion of the Conquistadors. Today the Palomino is a breed everyone recognizes because it can be most any breed at all, as long as it displays the trademark golden body and the white mane and tail. According to the Palomino Horse Breeders' Association, the color should be that of a U.S. fourteen-carat-gold coin. Roy Rogers' immortal Trigger was a Palomino Tennessee Walker. Many of the beautiful parade horses are Palomino Quarter Horses. Palominos are also found in many other breeds, including half-Arabians and Saddlebreds.

There are 66,000 registered Palomino Horses in America, in varying shades of gold, standing between 14 and 17 hands. Although Palominos are found in many different breeds, 50% of registered Palominos are Quarter Horses. The Palomino takes its name from the royal family in Spain, Palomina, but the Palomino Horses that Cortez brought to America in 1519 have been called Isabellas, after Queen Isabella. These highly treasured horses are seen across the United States in a wide variety of riding disciplines.

PHOTO © FAITH A. URIDEL

When God created the horse, he spoke to the magnificent creature: I have made thee without equal. All the treasures of this earth lie between thy eyes ... thou shalt fly without wings.

—*The Koran*

Where in this wide world can one find nobility without pride, friendship without envy or beauty without vanity? Here, where grace is laced with muscle and strength by gentleness confined.

—Ronald Duncan,
To The Horse

The Percheron of France is one of the most favored draft horses in the world due to its strength, durability, and pleasing appearance. Selective breeding using domestic stock and Belgian horses created the breed. While the more distant origins of the Percheron are not known precisely, it gains its name from the region of Le Perche, which lies southwest of Paris. The Percheron was among the earliest draft horses imported to America. The first shipment of five arrived from France in 1839. Breeders created the *Norman Stud Book* in 1876 and the name Percheron soon replaced Norman. More recently, the Percheron has been used as a circus horse, and many still recall a costumed performer on a big dapple gray as one of their favorite childhood memories.

The Percheron appears in only two colors, gray and black, though the animal may appear almost white with age. Stallions stand up to 17 hands, with the mares just slightly smaller. A mature Percheron may weigh close to a ton. The head is refined with rather large ears, wide-set eyes, and large, open nostrils. The neck is often thick with a long mane. The chest and body are substantial. The legs have good bone, as one may presume in a horse of this size, but unlike many of the draft breeds, they are clean, having little, if any, feather.

When Francisco Pizarro entered western South America to pillage the Incas in the 1500s, he brought with him 180 soldiers and 27 horses. The horses used by the Spanish formed the foundation of the breeds created in future centuries. One of the most distinctive breeds to emerge from South America is the Peruvian Paso. The Spanish term "Paso" means both "step" and "gently"—two terms which aptly describe the outstanding quality of the breed.

The Peruvian Paso has a straight or slightly concave profile with wide-set, expressive eyes. The neck is relatively short, arched, and muscular, and carries the head erect. The breed stands between 14.1 and 15.2 hands and weighs about 900 to 1200 pounds. The Paso has a short back and powerful chest and quarters and is naturally surefooted and agile. Its gait is energetic, although the temperament of the breed is quite gentle. The most distinguishing feature of the Peruvian Paso is its gait, or step, which is a lateral four-beat motion divided into Paso Ilano—a completely even, catlike four-beat gait—and Sobreandando—a slightly more lateral and faster four-beat gait. This breed possesses stamina and endurance and provides a smooth, smooth ride. It is found in various solid colors, often sorrel or chestnut, and excessive white is not favored. The mane and tail are allowed to grow long and full.

AT A PERUVIAN PASO SHOW YOU MAY SEE THE "CHAMPAGNE WALK." THIS IS A CROWD-PLEASING TEST OF THE HORSE'S SMOOTHNESS. THE RIDER WILL BALANCE A TRAY HOLDING A GLASS OF CHAMPAGNE ON THE FINGERTIPS OF ONE HAND. A HORSE WITH A SMOOTH GAIT WILL NOT CAUSE ONE DROP TO BE SPILLED.

PHOTO © SHARON EIDE

This most noble
beast is the most
beautiful, the
swiftest and of the
highest courage of
domesticated
animals. His long
mane and tail adorn
and beautify him.
He is of a fiery
temperament but
good natured,
obedient, docile and
well-mannered.

—Pedro Garcia Conde,
1685

When you are
on a great horse,
you have the
best seat you will
ever have.

—*Winston Churchill*

The Quarter Horse is truly an American breed of horse. It was created to compete in quarter-mile horse racing, one of the earliest forms of racing in the United States. While Galloways, Hobbies, Barbs, and Chickasaws influenced the early breed, the most influential stallion was a Thoroughbred named Janus, imported to America in 1756. He was a famous sire of great sprinters in Colonial America. The Quarter Horse proved capable of many tasks besides racing. When the pioneers moved westward, the Quarter Horse found a new role on the range where its agility and intelligence proved ideal for working cattle. The AQHA was formed in 1940, and the great champion Wimpy P-1 was given the prestigious #1 in the Registry. This was and is the breed of choice for rodeo riders, but the Quarter Horse is exceptionally versatile and is successful in any discipline where speed, agility, strength, and sense are valued. From reining and cutting to dressage and jumping, the American Quarter Horse is there, and winning.

This breed is recognized by its substantial muscle, good bone, short back, and deep body. The head is short, broad, full at the jowl and lighter at the muzzle, with small ears. The quarters are high and muscular, with great depth. Muscling remains strong through the hind leg across the thigh and gaskin. With 3.3 million horses registered, the Quarter Horse is one of the most popular horses in the world.

There is nothing better than the outside of a horse for the inside of a man.

—Old equine expression

Man does not rightly know the way to the heavenly world, but the horse does rightly know it.

—*Satapatha Brahmana XIII*

The tiny treasure of the Shetland Islands is a hardy soul whose rugged environment made him the pony he is today. The islands were rocky, bleak, and windswept. For many centuries, the Shetland lived in the open, protected from the elements only by its shaggy hair, long mane, and forelock. The islanders domesticated the ponies, using them to carry peat from the bogs, haul seaweed for fertilizer, and numerous other tasks. Later, the ponies were imported by Britain's miners for use in the coal mines. Some ponies literally never saw the light of day. While Shetlands stand only 9 to 10 hands and are usually measured in inches, relative to their size they are among the strongest of all breeds. They were first imported to America in 1885.

In the United States the Shetland Pony is still very popular, and we have also created a new breed called the American Shetland. This is a larger pony with the flashy action of the Hackney in harness. Found in almost every color imaginable, both ponies still carry the trademark abundant mane and tail.

Considered by many to be Britain's finest export, the Shire is descended from the Great Horse developed in the Middle Ages and later called the Old English Black Horse. Bred principally in Lincolnshire and Cambridgeshire, where the soil was deep and there was a need for considerable size and strength, the Shire became the largest and most powerful horse in Britain. It is used in America in pulling and plowing competitions, and in stylish teams.

The Shire is a horse of great size. A mature stallion may stand over 17 hands and weigh more than a ton. His heart girth is tremendous, easily measuring deeper than a man is tall. Mares and geldings are slightly less massive. This breed has large, wide-set and expressive eyes, and a rather convex nose. The shoulders are large and deep and the body has a substantial barrel. The legs are long with considerable feather. The Shire is usually found in bay, brown, black, and gray, with the traditional color being black with white feather.

The farmer was leading . . . a magnificent Shire, all of eighteen hands, with a noble head that he tossed proudly as he paced towards me. I appraised him with something like awe, taking in the swelling curve of the neck, the deep-chested body, the powerful limbs abundantly feathered above the massive feet.

—James Herriot,
Every Living Thing
(St. Martin's, 1992)

STANDARDBRED

The fastest harness horse in the world is the Standardbred. Tracing its ancestry back to Messenger, from the Darley Arabian line of Thoroughbreds, the foundation sire of the breed was called Hambletonian 10, and the top race for trotters bears this great sire's name. This American breed gains its name from the fact that a horse had to meet a certain "standard" in either breeding or in timed speed at the mile to be registered. In 1867, a gelding named Dexter trotted the mile in 2:19. In 1897, a pacer named Star Pointer reduced the time for a mile to 1:59. In 1904, the immortal Dan Patch paced the mile in 1:56. One of the greatest trotting records was set by the great gelding Greyhound in 1938; he ran the mile in 1:55.

"FOR A TROTTER TO BREAK THE TWO-MINUTE MILE BARRIER . . . MERELY ONCE IN A LIFETIME WOULD GIVE HIS OWNER CAUSE FOR PRIDE. TO BREAK IT SEVERAL TIMES WOULD GIVE HIM THE IMPRESSION OF OWNING A REAL CHAMPION. THE FREQUENCY AND REGULARITY WITH WHICH GREYHOUND KEPT AHEAD OF THE MAGIC MARK ON THE TIMEKEEPER'S CLOCK WAS ABSOLUTELY PHENOMENAL."

M. A. Stoneridge on Greyhound
Great Horses of Our Time
(Doubleday, 1972)

In many respects, the Standardbred resembles its ancestor the Thoroughbred. It does not stand as tall, averaging 15.2 hands, although it has a longer body. The quarters are sleek and muscular. The clean hind legs are set well back. The head may appear long and somewhat plain, but the Standardbred sees the world through honest, expressive eyes. Individual animals may either trot or pace. In the trot, diagonal pairs of legs work together; in the pace, legs on the same side move in pairs. While Standardbreds shine in the world of harness racing, many have found second careers as saddle horses where they are noted for their exceptional dispositions.

*...is in his movement—
the grand, bold,
sweeping, reaching
stride—that he gives the
feeling of beauty . . .*

—Marguerite Henry,
All About Horses
(Macmillan)

One of the three American gaited breeds, the Tennessee Walking Horse is famed for its flat-foot walk, running walk, and high, rolling canter. Before the Civil War, this horse was a comfortable ambler that was used for farm work of all kinds as well as family transportation. In 1886, Black Allen was foaled, an early Morgan and Standardbred cross that would become the foundation sire for a new breed. While Black Allen was expected to be a superior trotter, he was a failure at harness racing. Instead, he had a much more far-reaching fate; he was able to pass on his unique "way of going" to his offspring. These Walking Horses became the pride of Tennessee breeders. In 1914, an infusion of American Saddlebred blood, through the sire Giovanni, refined the breed, and in 1935, The Tennessee Walking Horse Breeders' Association was formed.

This is very much a "pretty is as pretty does" horse, known more for its outstanding gait and calm temperament than his physical attributes. There are no restrictions on color or markings. The popular roans of the 1940s were later replaced in favor by the sorrel with the flaxen mane and tail, and currently, blacks and other solid colors are most desirable. Standing 15 to 16 hands, this is a sturdy, sound breed as at home in the showring as on the family farm. The breed's character makes it a prized mount for children and beginners and it is widely recognized as a pleasure horse.

The Tennessee Stud was long and lean
the color of the sun
and his eyes were green
He had the nerve and he had the blood
and there never was a horse
like the Tennessee Stud.

—from the song "The Tennessee Stud"

Upon a courser,
whose delightful steps
Shall make the gazer
joy to see him tread.

—*Shakespeare*, Pericles

THOROUGHBRED

The Thoroughbred is one of the most brilliant and versatile horses bred in the world today. It is noted for its speed on the racetrack, but also has tremendous ability in hunting, polo, eventing, and jumping. The Thoroughbred has been used to create and refine other breeds. The key to the Thoroughbred's greatness is the speed and stamina for which it has been bred for over 300 years. The Thoroughbred originated in the late 1600s and early 1700s in Great Britain, where its Arabian ancestors—the Byerly Turk, the Godolphin Arabian, and the Darley Arabian—became the founding sires. The first Thoroughbred arrived in America in 1730 and was a Darley Arabian son named Bulle Rock.

The appearance of the Thoroughbred reveals its Arabian ancestry. It has a refined head with wide-set, intelligent eyes, a long, arched neck, and prominent withers. The shoulder is well sloped. The chest and heart girth are deep. The croup is high and the quarters powerful. The legs are clean and long with pronounced tendons. The coat is fine and silky. Its stride is long and low with incomparable speed. The Thoroughbred stands between 15 and 17 hands and is colored bay, chestnut, brown, black, and gray. Thoroughbreds are registered with The Jockey Club along with such luminaries as Exterminator, Man o' War, Citation, Native Dancer, Kelso, and Secretariat.

> *Take care not to vex the young horse, or cause it to abandon its affable gracefulness in disgust. For this is like the fragrance of blossoms, which never returns, once it has vanished.*
>
> —Antoine de la Baume Pluvinel

One of Europe's most famous breeds is the Trakehner. In the United States it is one of the most prized of the warmbloods. The breed originated with the founding of the Royal Trakehner Stud in East Prussia by Frederick William I in 1732. One of the great legends of history is the flight of the Trakehner from East Prussia during World War II. When the Russians invaded East Prussia after the collapse of the German army, 1,200 horses were herded on a 900-mile journey to the west that would last three months. Of those that survived, many were mares in foal. The incredible difficulties surmounted by these horses give ample testimony to the Trakehner's strength, spirit, and endurance. The Trakehner Verband was formed in West Germany in 1947 to continue the breed.

With superb conformation enhanced by an exemplary temperament, the Trakehner displays courage, strength, and stamina in the world of international sport. Its refined head shows the influence of Thoroughbred blood, and the Trakehner shows a unique character and expressiveness among the warmbloods. It has muscular, sloped shoulders and broad, powerful quarters. The legs are clean and strong. The breed appears in varying solid colors and stands 16 hands and over. Approved Trakehners will display the traditional elk-horn brand. This is a breed that makes an excellent jumping, dressage, and three-day-event horse.

And as I was riding along, my heart
resounded in the lawn-dampened steps,
resounded in the snorting and champing
on the bit by my gray, and a blissful
happiness lit up my heart and I knew:
If I now dropped out of the world,
I would fall into heaven.

— *Baron von Munchhausen*

A good horse is never a bad color.

—Old equine expression

PHOTO © GEMMA GIANNINI

Considered to be the most beautiful of ponies, the Welsh Mountain Pony is the oldest of the type, dating back to ancient times well before the Roman invasion. It is said that Julius Caesar began a stud for this breed near Lake Bala in Merionethshire. At one time it was used in Wales' coal mines, and in all its variations it is a well-formed, hardy animal. In 1902, The Welsh Pony and Cob Society was opened and is divided into four sections: Section A for the Welsh Mountain Pony, the original and smallest of the types, standing under 12 hands; Section B, The Welsh Pony that stands less than 13.2 hands; Section C for the Welsh Pony of Cob Type also standing under 13.2 hands but of the old type; and Section D, The Welsh Cob that stands over 13.2 hands. All of these types are descended from the Welsh Mountain Pony and show its influence.

The ears are small and erect above large, expressive eyes in a clean dished face. The body is compact with depth through the heart-girth and well-muscled quarters. The legs are usually clean with short, strong cannons, although some fine feather is permitted above tough, dense hooves. Most solid colors, such as blacks, bays, and chestnuts, are seen in the Welsh Ponies, with founding sire Dyoll Starlight responsible for much of the gray found in Section A. Palominos and duns are also found. This pony is an outstanding animal under saddle and in harness and makes an excellent partner for young people.

And God took a handful of southerly wind, blew His breath over it and created the horse.

—*Bedouin legend*

THE HORSE'S PRAYER

To Thee Master I offer my prayer; Feed me, water and care for me, and when the day's work is done, provide me with shelter, a clean dry bed, and a stall wide enough for me to lie down in comfort.

Always be kind to me. Talk to me, for your voice often means as much to me as the reins. Pet me sometimes, that I may serve you the more gladly and learn to love you. Do not jerk the reins, and do not whip me when going uphill. Never strike, beat or kick me when I do not understand what you want, but give me a chance to understand you. Watch me; and if I fail to do your bidding, see if something is wrong with my harness or feet.

I cannot tell you when I am thirsty so give me clean, cool water often. I cannot tell you in words when I am sick, so watch me, that by signs you may know my condition. Give me all possible shelter from the hot sun, and put a blanket on me, not when I am working, but when standing in the cold.

Never put a frosty bit in my mouth; first warm it by holding a moment in your hands.

I try to carry you and your burdens without a murmur, and wait patiently for you long hours of the day or night. Without the power to choose my shoes or path, I sometimes fall on the hard pavements which I have often prayed might be of such a nature as to give me a safe and sure footing. Remember that I must be ready at any moment to lose my life in your service.

And finally, O Master, when my useful strength is gone, do not turn me out to starve or freeze, or sell me to some cruel owner to be slowly tortured or starved to death; but do thou, my Master, take my life in the kindest way. And your God will reward you here and hereafter. You will not consider me irreverent if I ask this in the name of Him who was born in a stable. Amen.

Anonymous

BREED ASSOCIATIONS

American Miniature Horse
Association
5601 South I H 35W
Alverado, TX 76009
(817) 783-5600

American Saddlebred Horse
Association
4093 Ironworks Pike
Lexington, KY 40511
(606) 259-2742

International Andalusian and
Lusitano Horse Association
101 Carnoustie N., Suite 115
Shoal Creek, AL 35242
(205) 995-8900

Appaloosa Horse Club, Inc.
P.O. Box 8403
Moscow, ID 83843-0903
(208) 882-5578

International Arabian Horse Association
P.O. Box 33696
Denver, CO 80233-0696
(303) 450-4774

Belgian Draft Horse Corporation
of America
P.O. Box 335
Wabash, IN 46992-0335
(219) 563-3205

Clydesdale Breeders of the USA
17378 Kelley Rd.
Pecatonica, IL 61063
(815) 247-8780

American Connemara Pony Society
2630 Hunting Ridge Rd.
Winchester, VA 22603
(703) 662-5953, 722-ACPS

Friesian Horse Association of North
America
2023 Eastern Parkway
Louisville, KY 40204
(502) 459-5676

American Hackney Horse Society
4059 Iron Works Pike, Bldg. A
Lexington, KY 40511
(606) 255-8694

American Hanoverian Society
4059 Iron Works Pike
Lexington, KY 40511
(606) 255-4141

Lipizzan Association of North
America
P.O. Box 1133
Anderson, IN 46015
(317) 644-3904

Missouri Fox Trotting Horse Breed
Association
P.O. Box 1027
Ava, MO 65608-1027
(417) 683-2468

American Morgan Horse
Association
P.O. Box 960
Shelburne, VT 05482-0960
(802) 985-4944

American Paint Horse Association
P.O. Box 961023
Ft. Worth, TX 76161-0023
(817) 439-3400

Palomino Horse Breeders of
America
15253 E. Skelly Drive
Tulsa, OK 74116-2620
(918) 438-1234

Percheron Horse Association of
America
P.O. Box 141
Fredericktown, OH 43019-0141
(614) 694-3602

Peruvian Paso Horse
Registry of North America
1038 4th St., Suite 4
Santa Rosa, CA 95404-4319
(707) 579-4394

American Quarter Horse Association
P.O. Box 200
Amarillo, TX 79168
(806) 376-4811

American Shetland Pony Club
6748 North Frostwood Pkwy.
Peoria, IL 61615
(309) 691-9661

American Shire Horse Association
9251 Lansing Avenue North
Stillwater, MN 55082

United States Trotting Association
(Standardbred)
750 Michigan Avenue
Columbus, OH 43215-1191
(614) 224-2291

Tennessee Walking Horse
Breeders' and Exhibitors'
Association
P.O. Box 286
Lewisburg, TN 37091-0286
(615) 359-1574

The Jockey Club
(Thoroughbred)
821 Corporate Dr.
Lexington, KY 40503
(606) 224-2700

American Trakehner
Association
1520 West Church St.
Newark, OH 43055
(614) 344-1111

Welsh Pony and Cob Society
Of America
Box 2977
Winchester, VA 22604
(703) 667-6195

*I wish your
horses
swift and sure
of foot;
And so I do
commend you
to their backs.
Farewell.*

Shakespeare, Macbeth